Confident Happy Children

The book of A B C steps

by Jim Hickey

international peak performance coach

ISBN: 0-9926014-1-X   978-0-9926014-1-6

Published in Ireland by:

Your Ultimate Best Ltd.
Waters Edge, Barna, Galway

Illustrated by:
Rod St. Amant, Cypress, California

Printed and bound in Ireland by:
Standard Printers, Ballybrit Industrial Estate, Ballybrit Upper, Galway

A catalogue record of this book is available from the British Library.

Dedicated with love and gratitude to my wife Niamh and our two sons Josh and Rueben who keep on teaching me.

TESTIMONIAL

"This is a gem of a little book and I have no hesitation in recommending that it should be on the 'must read' list for all parents. The author places huge emphasis on the impact that language plays in all our lives, but especially in the day to day dialogue between parents and their children. It is obvious that he believes in the benefits of parents using a 'positive language framework' as a basis for communicating with their children. Little wonder then that every page is full of words of wisdom, positivity and sound advice. Also, throughout this lovely book Jim Hickey highlights the significance of good example, our children learn from us parents. We must make sure that at all times we provide them with good, positive example; this book provides the road map for parents to follow. I congratulate Jim on a really fabulous publication."

— **John Lonergan,**
Former Govenor of Mountjoy Prison

ACKNOWLEDGMENT

I would like to extend my hearfelt thanks to my family, my friends, all the people and families I have worked with, all the people who have shared their experiences with me, and to all the people who have assisted me in making this book happen, in particiular, Niamh Hickey, James Martin and Cathy Scanlon.

INTRODUCTION

This book came about from my passion to help our own sons grow up confident and happy.

As I looked into their cots when they were infants, I asked myself the question "what is the language I am going to use to help build their confidence and help them to be happy?"

I have always been fascinated with the huge effects of language, both negative and positive. For one negative it takes ten positives to override the negative.

Having being coached myself, years coaching people across the globe and through my continuous study; I have seen first hand the benefits of a 'positive language framework'.

I wrote Confident Happy Children, the ABC steps; to give parents a positive language system to help their children be confident, happy and secure.

— **Jim Hickey**

HOW TO USE THIS BOOK

Every parent is unique. Every child is unique. Every family situation is unique. There are no rules about how best to use this book. You can choose to focus on one letter a day for 26 days and then begin again. You can choose to start with one letter on the first day, two the next, then three and so on until you are going through the whole A - Z every day. Or, you can choose to cover A - Z every day.

However you choose to use this book I highly recommend reading the letters in sequence from A - Z. This helps both you and your child to remember and assimilate the important positive and affirming messages in each letter.

I also highly recommend that you make this book your own. Read it and reread it. Underline the parts that strike you and make notes on the pages. Digest every word, make them part of your everyday language. Integrate them into your own life so that you can lead by example and demonstrate to your children that thinking good thoughts really does have a beneficial impact on every aspect of life and that positive language is the most powerful language there is. Focus on the results you want, rather than on what you don't want.

Familiarize yourself with the concepts in this book until they are deeply ingrained in your mind and every word you speak is uplifting and empowering.

CONTENTS

FOREWORD

THE BENEFITS OF THE A-Z LIST OF MAGIC WORDS

How continuous positive reinforcement will help your child.

This is an amazing story of a Mum and Dad who spoke to their children, David and Jessie, in a very special way from a very young age. The parents created a simple system that they called the 'I AM – YOU ARE list of magic words' to say to their children, in order to instill powerful language and thus powerful positive emotions in their children. The outcome of this approach is to support the child in all areas of development.

CHAPTER 1

PREPARATION

Prepare to be the best parent you can be

Firstly, the Mum and Dad created a 'communication "magic" checklist' for themselves that they committed to reading daily, to help condition themselves to a higher standard of parenting and communication with their children.

This is their list...

A

We prepare to teach our children through acknowledging their presence and greatness each morning. We greet them with 'Good Morning' each and every morning and continue to acknowledge them throughout the day. We prepare never to take them for granted .

ACKNOWLEDGE

B

We prepare to teach our children by first 'BUILDING' on their strengths. We praise their greatness and champion their successes both big and small. We say things like.....That's amazing! That's brilliant! That's cool! Fantastic! Well Done!

BUILD

C

We prepare to teach
our children by clearing our minds
and letting go of any personal issues so
we can enter their world, see everything
through their eyes and be aware of
their view of the world.

19

D

We prepare to teach our children by developing their awareness, and teaching them to be responsible, kind, courageous, honourable, respectful and mannerly. We prepare to support their progress and allow them to grow, have fun and enjoy their precious lives. We also need to let them learn from their mistakes. Letting our children learn from their mistakes helps build resilience in them.

DEVELOP

20

We prepare to teach our
children by 'EXAMPLE', by being the best
parents we can be! We will apologise to each other
when we are wrong if we want our children to apologise
to each other when they are wrong. We will eat healthy
food if we want our children to eat healthy food. We will
exercise our bodies if we want our children to exercise.
We will lead by 'EXAMPLE' in everything we
want our children to be and do.

F

We prepare to teach our children through 'FEEDBACK'. We will repeat back to them what they say; this will build rapport and will show the children that they are being listened to. This will make our children more aware of what they are saying and will improve their communication skills and their language skills. Overall this will promote their self-confidence.

FEEDBACK

We prepare to teach our children by 'GIVING THEM TIME'. We will go down to their height level when we speak to them. We will become aware that these times of connection and love are the 'magic moments' that we and our children will remember in years to come. It was once asked of a child how to spell love and he answered - T.I.M.E.

GIVING

23

H

We prepare to
'HUG' our children and ask
them for hugs, knowing that these
loving connections will make our
children feel safe. When hugging is
practiced daily, it will become a
lifetime habit.

HUG

I

We prepare to teach our children through 'INTUITION'. We pay attention and notice the things that are not being said.

INTUITION

J

We prepare to teach
our children through 'journalling' by
writing down, recording and taking photos
as much as possible. By doing this, children
will learn how to stack their "magic moments".
Reflecting, recording and recalling the
magic moments is the key to integrating
happiness.

JOURNAL

K

We prepare to speak 'KIND' and loving words to our children and ask them to speak kind and loving words to us and to each other.

KIND

27

L

We prepare
to 'LISTEN' carefully to
what our children are
actually saying.

LISTEN

28

We prepare
ourselves by 'MIRRORING' and
matching our children's voice tones
and pace of speaking which will
enhance our rapport, and improve
our communication with them.

MIRRORING

N

We prepare to teach our children, by knowing what their 'NEEDS' are and meeting them. If they are looking for attention we will give it to them as we know that the two things we all need most are, to be 'loved' and to feel that we are 'good enough'.

NEEDS

We prepare to teach our children through offering them 'OPTIONS'. We will give them choices at all times. In this way they will feel responsible for their own situations. They will come to learn that they have a choice in how they behave which will ultimately reflect the situation they find themselves in. We praise and reward them when they make good responsible decisions.

31

P

We prepare to teach our
children through 'POSITIVE ANTICIPATION'.
We will say things like "This is going to be the best day
of our lives! This is going to be a super happy fun day" ...
before their day even starts. We will teach them through
questioning " ... what kind of day are you going to have ?" • • •
this will allow them ownership over what kind of day they
anticipate having. This will also help our children to plan
their days which will help them prepare for, expect
and create excitement in the day ahead.

POSITIVE
Anticipation

We prepare to teach
our children through 'questioning'
rather than 'telling' them what to do. We
will ask them "Would you?, Could you?,
Can you?, How could you?, What is most
important right now?"

QUESTIONING

33

R

We prepare to teach our children through reflection by asking them questions such as, what went well? What didn't? What could you do even better?

34

REFLECTION

We prepare to teach
our children to exercise and develop
their smiling muscle though smiling with
their full face and by smiling back at them.
We will ask the question "who has the biggest
smile today?" We will guide and encourage
them to continue smiling and enjoy
themselves immensely.

T

We prepare to teach
our children to be truthful at all
times, we teach them to share the truth
and to live by the truth. We praise and
reward them when they share the truth
and teach them that what they give out
they will get back in life.

36

TRUTHFUL

U

We prepare to
teach out children through
understanding them with
empathy.

UNDERSTANDING

37

V

We prepare to teach our children to understand their values. We will make them aware of their values by asking them what is most important to them and what are their passions. We will help them understand how their values will guide and shape their decisions, throughout their lives. We will guide and check in with them regularly.

VALUES

We prepare to teach our children through warmth and trust, as it is the most effective way for open and honest communication.

WARMTH

39

X

We prepare
to teach our children to see
the 'x factor' in themselves by
letting ourselves get excited
with our children.

X-FACTOR

40

Y

We prepare
to teach our children
through asking them to say
'yes' and to celebrate their
wonderful lives.

YES

41

Z

We prepare to teach our children to be present and in the Zone.

ZONE

In their own lives the Mum and Dad knew "that we ARE who we say we are" and that its important to direct their children's minds in a most positive way in terms of who they tell themselves they are.

CHAPTER 2

A-Z LIST OF MAGIC WORDS

Nurture your children to be the best they can be

Mum and Dad then put together this brilliant list of wonderful words and created a simple A – Z system for David and Jessie. They knew it would be an easy way for them all to learn. As they repeated these words daily they would become part of their language and part of their life and bring happiness to all. Mum and Dad would lead by saying "I AM" and "YOU ARE' as they knew the best way to teach is to lead first and that all children look to their parents first for guidance.

They also knew that using this A to Z list of magic words would become part of their family identity. They explained this to David and Jessie and they reinforced their teaching in picture form with simple drawings of matchstick people.

This is what they did...

47

51

61

63

64

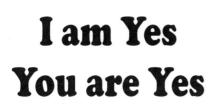

When they finished their words of A – Z, they celebrated in order to physically integrate the process. They all jumped for joy and shouted YAY!

Mum and Dad explained to David and Jessie that this celebration was very important as it instilled and integrated the feeling of joy, which anchored all these powerful words into their nervous system. They taught David and Jessie that they learn more when they are excited. It was apparent to Mum and Dad that David and Jessie enjoyed being surrounded by this language and they saw how it helped their happiness grow. They explained to the children that our words become our world.

CHAPTER 3

THANK YOU!

End each day with gratitude for everybody,
everything and every experience

At the end of each day, at bedtime, Mum and Dad recited these words of gratitude to David and Jessie to heighten their awareness of and appreciation for all that happened that day.

This is what they said:

77

B

79

D

80

81

83

84

85

86

87

89

91

93

94

95

97

98

99

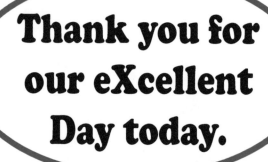

The End

PS: We Live What We Learn

If we learn to be Amazing
We live to be Amazing

If we learn to be Brilliant
We live to be Brilliant

If we learn to be Confident
We live to be Confident

If we learn to be Delighted
We live to be Delighted

If we learn to be Excited
We live to be Excited

If we learn to be Fun
We live to be Fun

If we learn to be Grateful
We live to be Grateful

If we learn to be Happy
We live to be Happy

If we learn to be Incredible
We live to be Incredible

If we learn to be Joyful
We live to be Joyful

If we learn to be Kind
We live to be Kind

If we learn to Listen
We live to Listen

If we learn to be Magical
We live to be Magical

If we learn to be Nice
We live to be Nice

If we learn to be Open Hearted
We live to be Open Hearted

If we learn to be Positive
We live to be Positive

If we learn to be Quality
We live to be Quality

If we learn to be Remarkable
We live to be Remarkable

If we learn to be Smiling
We live to be Smiling

If we learn to be Truthful
We live to be Truthful

If we learn to be Unique
We live to be Unique

If we learn to be Vibrant
We live to be Vibrant

If we learn to be Wonderful
We live to be Wonderful

If we learn to be eXcellent
We live to be eXcellent

If we learn to be Yes
We live to be Yes

If we learn to be in the Zone
We live to be in the Zone